NATIONAL
GEOGRAPHIC

A SUBURBAN
COMMUNITY
of the 1950s

GARE THOMPSON

PICTURE CREDITS
Cover © Wood River Gallery/PictureQuest; pages 1, 6 (top), 12, 13 H. Armstrong Roberts, Philadelphia, PA; pages 2-3 © 2000 Mike Wallen-Coolstock.com; pages 4-5 Shelly Grossman/FPG; page 6 (left) AJ's Sports Stop, Vienna, VA; pages 6 (right), 10, 17, 18-19 Superstock; page 7 Archive Photos, NY; page 8 (top) © 2000 Michael Witzel-Coolstock.com; pages 8 (bottom), 16 Photo copied by Joe Ferlise, Courtesy Levittown Public Library; pages 9, 15 Lambert/Archive Photos, NY; page 11 (top) Culver Pictures, Inc, NY; page 11 (bottom) © Bettmann/CORBIS; page 14 Popperfoto/Archive Photos, NY; page 14 (insets) Blank Archives/Archive Photos, NY; page 15 (center) Hake's Americana & Collectibles, York, PA; page 15 (bottom) Courtesy Vlasic Foods, International; pages 16 (top & inset), 18 (center & bottom) Photodisc; page 18 (top) The Everett Collection, NY; page 20 National Archives-Coolstock.com; page 21 Photo Courtesy of Tupperware Corporation; pages 22-23 Schwinn Cycling & Fitness, Inc.; 22 © 2000 Ron Saari-Coolstock.com; page 24 Courtesy Funk & Junk at http://www.funkandjunk.com, Alexandria, VA; Back cover (top to bottom) Used with permission of the Board of Trustees of the New Bedford Free Public Library; T. H. Benton and R. P. Benton Testamentary Trusts/Licensed by VAGA, New York, NY; Brown Brothers, Sterling, PA; Culver Picturs, NY; © Brenda Tharp/Photo Researchers, Inc., NY

MAP
National Geographic Society

Produced through the worldwide resources of the National Geographic Society, John M. Fahey, Jr., President and Chief Executive Officer; Gilbert M. Grosvenor, Chairman of the Board; Nina D. Hoffman, Executive Vice President and President, Books and Education Publishing Group

PREPARED BY NATIONAL GEOGRAPHIC SCHOOL PUBLISHING
Ericka Markman, Senior Vice President and President Children's Books and Education Publishing Group; Steve Mico, Vice President, Editorial Director; Marianne Hiland, Executive Editor; Anita Schwartz, Project Editor; Tara Peterson, Editorial Assistant; Jim Hiscott, Design Manager; Linda McKnight, Art Director; Diana Bourdrez, Anne Whittle, Photo Research; Matt Wascavage, Manager of Publishing Services; Sean Philpotts, Production Manager; Jane Ponton, Production Artist.

MANUFACTURING AND QUALITY MANAGEMENT
Christopher A. Liedel, Chief Financial Officer; Phillip L. Schlosser, Director; Clifton M. Brown III, Manager.

PROGRAM DEVELOPMENT
Gare Thompson Associates, Inc.

Published by the National Geographic Society
1145 17th Street, N.W.
Washington, D.C. 20036-4688

ISBN: 0-7922-8691-X

Fourth Printing July, 2004
Printed in Canada.

Table of Contents

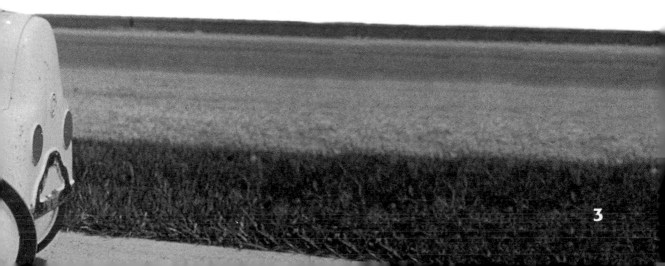

In 1945 World War II was over. The men and women serving in the military came home to their families. Often, these young families had to live with their parents.

Abraham Levitt and his two sons, William and Alfred, had an idea. They wanted to build houses that these young families could buy. The houses had to be cheap but well-made. So the Levitts bought land on Long Island in New York. They built simple homes. All the homes looked alike. The homes all sold for the same low price.

Young families waited in lines to buy the homes. Soon a new town just outside of New York City was born. It was called Levittown. It was a **suburban** community.

The Golden family—Samuel, his wife Barbara, their daughter Rachel, and son Aaron—wanted the "American Dream." They wanted their own home. They were living with Samuel Golden's parents. The family apartment in Brooklyn, New York, was crowded. The young Golden family saved their money and bought a home in Levittown. This is their story.

CHAPTER 1

Our Brooklyn Neighborhood, *1953*

It is a hot summer. My name is Aaron Golden. I live in Brooklyn, New York. It's the best place to live because it's the home of the Brooklyn Dodgers. They are the best baseball team ever. The Dodgers are much better than the Yankees even if they haven't won the World Series yet. It's only 1953. I know they'll win soon.

When a game is on the radio, we all sit outside on the **stoop.** It's like a small porch outside our front door. My grandfather turns up the radio loud. It seems like the whole neighborhood is on our stoop. My grandmother passes out cookies. My parents and their friends talk about politics or work. When the game starts, it's silent. Even my ten-year-old sister, Rachel, knows to be quiet. After all, no one wants to miss Jackie Robinson getting a hit. He's my favorite player.

Baseball trading card
▼

JACKIE ROBINSON 3b of BROOKLYN DODGERS

Our apartment is crowded and noisy. Seven people live here. We only have five rooms. I'd like to have my own room. Now, I sleep on the couch in the living room. In the morning, everyone wakes me up.

Grandmother is the first one up. She makes breakfast. She says it's the most important meal. She even makes my dad eat. He's always running for work. He works in a bank. He goes to school at night. The government is paying for him to go to school because he fought in the war.

My mom cooks lunch. Of course, my grandmother has to add to the menu. My mother just smiles. She says food is like love to Grandma. The more we eat, the more we're loved. Rachel and I are just glad Grandma's a good cook.

My parents have been talking a lot at night. Some of their friends have bought homes on Long Island. Grandpa says it's too far away. Why move? I think my parents want their own home.

I am not sure I want to move. I'd miss my friends. I walk to school. It's two streets over from where we live. I can come home for lunch or go to Uncle Max's diner.

Dad asks me if I'd like my own room. Well, sure I would. Mom keeps looking at these magazines full of pictures of furniture. She clips out recipes, too. She keeps saying that she'd love to have her own kitchen.

Grandma says that Long Island is the end of the world. She'd miss us. How could she visit? Mom says she would learn to drive and would pick Grandma up. Grandfather says cars cost a lot of money. Furniture costs money, too.

I wonder if the kids there like the Dodgers. Tomorrow, my parents are going to look at this place called Levittown. It has houses that are cheap. My grandmother says that you get what you pay for. Dad sighs.

▶ **People camped outside the Levitt office to sign up for Levitt homes.**

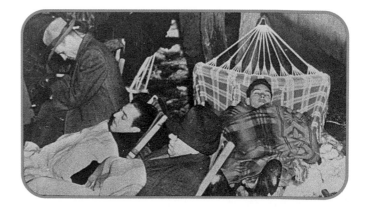

CHAPTER 2

Moving to Levittown

My parents are excited. They loved the houses in Levittown. Mom says that the houses are called ranches. I ask if it's like the Wild West. She says no. She shows me a picture. The house looks nice. It is yellow.

Grandma is quiet. She says she has been saving some money for us. Now is the time to give it to us. Dad and Grandpa talk about how much the house costs. It costs $9,500. That sounds like a lot of money to me.

Dad says he will be able to take the train to work and school. Mom says she will sew curtains. The house has a washing machine. Grandpa says that Dad can have his tools. Dad can fix anything.

Rachel and I are sad. We must say goodbye to our friends. We will have to go to a new school. I hope I like it. I wonder if Levittown has a library. I like to read.

9

Mom and Dad bought a house! Dad says it was so easy. They met with the man selling the house. They signed a **contract.** The house is ours. We are moving.

The people in the neighborhood give a party for us. Everyone brings gifts. Grandma gives Mom some pots. Mrs. Donovan gives us a bit of Irish lace for good luck. Uncle Max gives us lots of food for our new refrigerator. The Tortellis give us a cookbook for the **barbecue**.

Dad says that he will build a bookcase in my bedroom. He will build a dollhouse for Rachel. We talk to our friends. We all make plans to visit.

Grandpa tells us to walk our friends to the street. On the street, there is a car with a red bow on it. It is from Grandpa and Grandma. They hug us and laugh. Grandma tells us that now we have to visit. Grandpa says it's an old car, but it works. Mom sits behind the wheel. Everyone laughs. Tomorrow we move.

From above, Levittown looks like a maze of houses.

Today is bright and sunny. We load Uncle Max's truck. Dad found a store that sold used furniture. We bought beds. The house already has **appliances** like a refrigerator and a stove. Soon we are ready to go. I wave goodbye to my friends. It feels like we are going far away, but it's only an hour away. Dad says we'll come back for baseball games. I hope so. Rachel starts to cry. Mom gives her a hug. They settle into the car. Grandma and Grandpa are in the car, too. I ride with Uncle Max.

We arrive in Levittown. Dad gets lost. It is a **maze** of houses. The roads go round and round. The houses all look alike, except for the colors. Ours is yellow, but so are many of the other houses. People are working on their lawns. They wave to us. Finally we find our house.

Grandma says that the house is small, but neat. She thinks there's enough room for the four of us. But there won't be enough room if she and Grandpa want to stay over. I tell her she can have my room.

A huge window fills most of the back wall. Mom says she will plant flowers in the backyard. Grandpa says it is like having the outside inside. Dad says maybe we can plant a few vegetables, too. Grandma says I'll have to learn how to mow the lawn!

I like the fireplace. It has a **mantel** on it. We can put pictures of the Dodgers there. Mom says maybe we'll put those pictures in my room. Dad and Grandpa look in the **attic.** The attic will make an extra room. It will be mine.

Mom likes the kitchen in the front of the house. She can watch us through the window. We race out into the yard. A yard! We run around.

While we are in the yard, the doorbell rings. It is a Welcome Wagon lady. She gives Mom a package to welcome us to the neighborhood.

This neighborhood is different from our neighborhood in Brooklyn. In Brooklyn, everything was a block or two away. Here you have to drive to get things. But we do have a yard. I think that we will like it here in our new home, Levittown.

CHAPTER 3

Settling in the Community, 1954

We've been here a year. I love having my own room. It's like being at the top of a castle. Rachel and I have made friends. We play baseball. Dad coaches my Little League team. Rachel takes dance lessons. She had her first **recital** in May. She was good.

Rachel has a lot of sleepovers. Who needs a lot of girls in the house? My friends and I camp out in the backyard. We have tents. It's neat. It's hard to tell where our backyard ends and our neighbors' begin. Mom says that it's a good thing we all get along. We have barbecues and picnics.

We also joined one of the nine pools here. We have to wear rubber bathing caps. I still miss running through the spraying fire hydrants in Brooklyn. Tommy Murphy came to visit. He loved the pool. I let him ride my bike, too.

Dodger fans and game tickets

We all root for the Dodgers here. My friends and I listen to the games on the radio. Sometimes Dad drives us out to Ebbets Field. It's great to see the games. I think that the Dodgers will win the World Series.

On the bus ride to school we all talk about baseball. It's fun riding the bus. I don't like bringing my lunch. I miss Uncle Max's diner. All the other kids bring lunch, too. What I really like about Levittown is the library. They have great programs. We have read-alouds and plays. It's a fun place to be on a rainy day.

Mom is learning to drive. Dad is teaching her. She wants to use the car while Dad is at work. She'll drive him to the train. Then we'll all pick him up. She's doing fine. Well, except when she hit our neighbor's trashcan. Grandma says maybe she'll learn to drive, too. Grandpa says he won't teach her. Maybe Mom will. Mom wants to be able to drive to the grocery store and to the department store.

At night, we watch television after supper. Our favorite show is *Lassie*. I'd love to get a collie just like Lassie. What a great dog! Tonight we are going to eat TV dinners. The meal is turkey with gravy, mashed potatoes, and peas. It looks pretty good. We'll watch TV and eat!

Dad reads home improvement magazines. They have lots of ideas on how to fix up our house. We now have a **patio** area where we barbecue. Our neighbor helped Dad build it.

The house looks nice. We have curtains that Mom made. Mom's a good cook. She makes a lot of things with Jell-O®. Grandma thinks that Jell-O® is not a dessert, but we like it. I like it best made with fruit and marshmallows.

Mom drives now. Some days Mom and her friends work at the school. Mom is president of the PTA. She also **volunteers** at the library and the local hospital. She is always busy.

CHAPTER 4

Community Life, 1955

This is the year the Dodgers will win the World Series. So far they are doing great. The Yankees are doing well, too. I know we can win. It's all we talk about at school. Dad says everyone on the train is talking about the World Series. Mom says that they talk about it at her card parties, too.

Rachel is now taking piano lessons. I take them, too. School is fun here. We have to study hard, but we do neat things, too. Last week we went to the Museum of Natural History in New York City.

Levittown has grown. It now has three churches and a synagogue. Lots of stores are nearby. We have our own post office. We even have a restaurant. A bowling alley opened up down the road. Friday nights we bowl. Mom is joining the women's league. Dad will join the men's league. Bowling is almost as much fun as baseball.

We all celebrate the Fourth of July. There's a barbecue in every backyard. You can just walk from yard to yard eating. After it gets dark, we'll have fireworks. Dad likes Memorial Day better. On Memorial Day, Dad and his friends wear their old military uniforms. They march in a huge parade. Most of the men here fought in World War II.

▲

**A scene
from *The
Honeymooners***

The Dodgers are in the World Series! They're playing the Yankees. They have to win this year! Dad hurries home from work so we can listen to the games. Finally, they win! In the seventh and last game, they beat the Yankees by two runs! The Dodgers are the world champions! Everyone starts cheering. You can hear the neighbors yelling. Grandpa calls us from Brooklyn. We will have a big party to celebrate!

This Halloween two kids came by who were lost. They thought that our house was their house! Luckily, Mom knew where they lived. They lived in a yellow house just like ours, but it was two streets over.

Dad finished his latest project. He added a sun room. It's like a porch. Grandma likes to sit there. She says no bugs can get to her and it's cool. In the summer, we move the TV there. Our favorite show now is *The Honeymooners*. It's about people from Brooklyn. Next, Dad wants to turn the **carport** into a garage. Mom thinks he's going to run out of space before he runs out of projects.

Yesterday Dad was mowing our lawn. Who should drive up but Mr. Levitt, the builder of Levittown. He was sitting in his big Cadillac with a **chauffeur** driving it. What a great car! Mr. Levitt likes to check on people's lawns. If your grass is too high, he'll tell you to cut it.

On Thanksgiving Day our whole family is going to the football game. This will be the third year the high school is playing. I hope they win. If the Dodgers can win, so can our high school! After the game, we'll have a turkey dinner with all the trimmings.

Next spring Mom is going to run the garden tour. People pay to go on the tour. The money is used to help our school. There will be ten gardens on the tour. Mom's garden will be one of them. She is very proud of her lilacs and tulips. I hope they'll look good.

Grandma and Grandpa visit us often. They like to come to our parties. Even Uncle Max visits us. He thinks Dad's tomatoes are great. I'm glad we moved here.

CHAPTER 5

The Suburbs, *1958*

People are still moving here. Levittown is becoming a big town. The town had to build a new high school for all the new students. Each year it seems as though my classes are bigger. We have lots of stores near us. Mom says she doesn't have to go into the city for anything. Everything she wants is right here. Dad works at the local bank. He drives to work. He says he likes it better than taking the train into New York City.

We have two cars now. Mom is working so she needs a car, too. I work mowing people's lawns and shoveling snow. Dad has been teaching me how to build things. Our house has a porch, a garage, and a sun room. Each time Dad's magazines come, Mom groans.

◄ **Women arrive for a Tupperware® party.**

I am in high school now. Rachel is president of her class. We both help out at the library on weekends. I still love books. I play football. I still ride my bike to school. I can't wait until I learn to drive. If mom gives me her car, I'll treat her to lunch at the nearby drive-in.

Some of Mom's friends sell makeup or things for the kitchen. They hold a special "party." At the party, women buy plastic food containers or makeup. Mom says it's a good way for women to make money.

Many of our neighbors now work in local stores. Some people are even starting their own businesses. A friend of Dad's started a building company. At first it was just him and one worker. Now he has ten people who work for him. A lot of building is going on here on Long Island.

Grandma and Grandpa say that Brooklyn is changing, too. Many of the families we knew best have moved away. The Murphys and the Tortellis are gone. Uncle Max is selling his diner. He doesn't know all his customers the way he used to. The neighborhood grocery store is closing. People want to shop in big supermarkets. And the Dodgers have left Brooklyn. No one gathers on the stoop to listen to the games anymore.

Grandma and Grandpa come to visit us more often now. Mom taught Grandma to drive. Grandma even makes a Jell-O® dessert. Grandpa and Uncle Max help Dad with his vegetables. Dad built flower boxes for our windows. Mom likes them. I made one for Grandma.

Kids still ride bikes all over Levittown. Soon, I'll be driving. Well, I will if Mom lets me borrow her car. She said she'll teach me. Dad said he would. I think I'll take the driving course at school. Levittown is a good place to live. As Dad says, we live the American Dream here.

Levittown continued to grow. The Levitts built other towns like Levittown. Levittown became a model for suburban communities. Today, Levittown is still there. Recently, it celebrated the fiftieth anniversary of its founding. Some of the first people to buy a home in Levittown still own and live in the same house.

Aaron went to City College. He studied law. He became a lawyer and worked in New York City. He lived in a small apartment in the city. It seemed as small as his old room. Aaron married a girl from Brooklyn. They moved to Long Island, not far from Levittown.

Rachel went to City College, too. She became a music teacher. She married a boy from Levittown. They moved to Westchester, a suburb of New York City.

Sam and Barbara still live in Levittown. Their house is now finished. At least Sam says that until he gets another magazine. Grandma and Grandpa moved to Florida. The Golden family all watch the Los Angeles Dodgers on television. But Aaron says there will never be a player better than Jackie Robinson.

Glossary

appliance – a household machine, such as a refrigerator or a washing machine

attic – the space just below the roof of a house

barbecue – a charcoal grill used for cooking food outdoors

carport – an open-sided shelter for an automobile

chauffeur – a person whose work is driving someone else's automobile

contract – a legal agreement

mantel – a wooden or stone shelf above a fireplace

maze – a confusing series of paths through which people may have a hard time finding their way

patio – a paved area next to a house, used for relaxing or eating outdoors

recital – a musical performance

stoop – a small porch with stairs at the entrance of a house

suburban – an area next to or near a city

volunteer – to offer to do a job, usually without pay